Preamble
LEADERSHIP

Bob —
Thank you for inviting me to Memphis!

Debra

Preamble
LEADERSHIP

A Leader's Guide to
Building a Legacy Culture

Delise Simmons

PALMETTO
PUBLISHING
Charleston, SC
www.PalmettoPublishing.com

Copyright © 2024 by Delise Simmons

All rights reserved

No portion of this book may be reproduced, stored in a retrieval system, or transmitted in any form by any means—electronic, mechanical, photocopy, recording, or other—except for brief quotations in printed reviews, without prior permission of the author.

Paperback ISBN: 979-8-8229-5985-9

"We the People of the United States, in order to form a more perfect Union, establish Justice and ensure domestic Tranquility, provide for the common Defense, promote the general Welfare, secure the Blessings of Liberty to ourselves and our Posterity. Do ordain and establish this Constitution for the United States of America."

CONTENTS

Foreword — xi

Chapter 1: We the People — 1

The Foundation of Preamble Leadership — 1
The Essence of "We the People" — 3
We the People Success Stories — 4
Strategies for creating We the People — 5
We the People Exercises — 6
We the People Summary — 7

Chapter 2: A More Perfect Union — 9

The Art of Alignment — 9
The Importance of Cultural Fit — 9
A More Perfect Union Success Stories — 11
Strategies for Achieving a Perfect Cultural Union — 12
Exercise: The Cultural Fit Workshop — 14
A More Perfect Union Summary — 16

Chapter 3: Establish Justice — 17

Defining Your Company's Value System — 17
The Role of Core Values — 17
Establish Justice Success Stories — 19
Strategies to Identifying and Defining Core Values — 20
Exercise: The Values Workshop — 21
Establish Justice Summary — 24

Chapter 4:   Ensure Domestic Tranquility — 25

Fostering a Positive Work Environment — 25
The Importance of Employee Well-Being — 26
Ensure Domestic Tranquility Success Stories — 27
Strategies for Promoting Employee Well-Being — 28
Exercise: The Well-Being Assessment — 30
Ensure Domestic Tranquility Summary — 31

Chapter 5:   Provide for the Common Defense — 33

Building Resilient Teams and Systems — 33
The Dual Nature of Competition — 33
Provide for the Common Defense Success Stories — 35
Strategies for Defending Against Competition — 36
Exercise: The SWOT Analysis Workshop — 37
Provide for the Common Defense Summary — 39

Chapter 6:   Promote the General Welfare — 41

Creating a Thriving Workplace and Being a Good Neighbor — 41
The Interconnectedness of Workplace and Community — 41
Promote the General Welfare Success Stories — 43
Exercise: The Community Impact Workshop — 45
Promote the General Welfare Summary — 47

Chapter 7:   Secure the Blessings of Liberty — 49

Empowering Employees and Fostering a Culture of Autonomy — 49
The Strength of Empowerment — 49
Secure the Blessings of Liberty Success Stories — 51
Strategies for Empowering Employees — 52
Exercise: The Empowerment Audit — 53
Secure the Blessings of Liberty Summary — 55

Chapter 8: To Ourselves and Our Posterity — 57

Building a Sustainable and Enduring Legacy — 57
The Importance of a Sustainable Legacy — 58
To Ourselves and our Posterity Success Stories — 59
Strategies for Building a Sustainable Legacy — 60
Exercise: The Legacy Blueprint Workshop — 62
To Ourselves and our Posterity Summary — 63

Chapter 9: Do Ordain and Establish — 65

The Preamble Leadership Approach — 65
The Roadmap to Integration — 66

Conclusion — 71

Resources — 73

Exercise: Legacy Visioning Workshop — 73

Employee Wellness Assessment — 75

Physical Well-Being — 75
Psychological Well-Being — 76
Occupational Well-Being — 78
Scoring Rubric for Employee Wellness Assessment — 79
Total Score Calculation — 80
Interpretation of Scores — 80
Overall Wellness (Out of 75) — 81
Using the Results — 81

Company Empowerment Practices Assessment   83

1. Leadership Commitment   83
2. Decision-Making Autonomy   84
3. Access to Information   84
4. Training and Development   84
5. Recognition and Rewards   85
6. Feedback Mechanisms   85
7. Culture of Trust   86
8. Cross-Functional Collaboration   86
9. Inclusive Practices   87
10. Measurement and Improvement   87

Foreword

Delise and I have worked together from our early days at Southwest Airlines to helping build JetBlue Airways... and many other stops along the way!

This book is a perfect read for anyone who truly wishes to exponentially improve their culture and overall performance. Having worked for decades with Delise, I can attest to her innate ability to positively influence culture around the set of customized values and behaviors and then to use a model she was a partner in creating to assess your progress. Her life's work has been in the area of building strong people-centric cultures that show a return to both team members at all levels and investors. She is one of those rare talents that also is an exceptional communicator and operator and confirms both in this great read, "Preamble Leadership."

Ann Rhoades
President, PeopleInk
www.peopleink.com

CHAPTER 1:

We the People

I grew up in the 1970s where on Saturday mornings, "Schoolhouse Rock" was always blaring on the television in our living room. For those of you who are not familiar, the program was an animated, educational series aimed at teaching children subjects such as history, science, and math using songs and short stories. One of the songs that always rang in my head was the Schoolhouse Rock rendition of The Preamble to the Constitution of the United States. It was catchy enough that 40 years later, I can still recite the Preamble as if I wrote it. The Constitution that now hangs in the National Archives Museum in Washington D.C. can still serve to guide us in how we assemble our organizations to make them strong!

The Foundation of Preamble Leadership

In the Preamble, the opening words, "We the People," are not merely a statement; they are a powerful declaration of collective unity and shared purpose. In the business realm, it translates into an understanding that your organization is built upon the strength of every person you hire. These words encapsulate a vision where every individual contributes to the greater good, where each voice matters, and where the collective effort is greater than the sum of its parts. Some of the best companies I have had the privilege to work with have been similarly constructed.

From the years 1989 to 1997, I had the great good fortune to work in the People Department at Southwest Airlines in Dallas, Texas. During that time, the airline was ranked as one of the "Top Ten Places to Work in America." I learned about culture and leadership and how structure has so much influence over both of those. We created the Southwest Airlines' University for People, where we helped establish the values and behaviors for Southwest, which stood as our own "Constitution." It was here I learned how important leaderships' role in leading from a place of values really is. In the realm of leadership and company culture, this concept is paramount. For a company to thrive, its culture must be built on its principles. Of the People. For the People. By the People. (We called our Human Resources Department the People Department for that specific reason!)

In a recent conversation with Shari Conaway, who recently retired as the Managing Director of the People Department at Southwest Airlines, I asked her why she believed the airline has been able to maintain such a strong culture over its fifty years of service. Her answer was, "it began with the way Southwest was created. We started off as warriors, a fledgling airline trying to make its mark. We never lost that warrior spirit, even as we grew." That is the embodiment of "We the People."

The Essence of "We the People"

In the corporate world, "We the People" translates to recognizing that every employee, from the C-suite to the front line, plays a vital role in shaping the company's culture. I define culture as "a collection of the behaviors of the people within a team, group, or organization." A company's culture is not dictated from the top down; it is a living, breathing entity that evolves with the contributions of all its members. It changes with every hire. Each person we bring into our company can either enhance or dilute our company culture. If we choose well and make a good culture match in hiring, we enhance the culture. If we choose poorly, or perhaps through poor design of a merger/acquisition, we dilute the culture. Either way, our culture is fluid and needs consistent attention for it to grow in the direction we choose. Leadership drives the culture by creating the framework for the values, behaviors, and direction of the organization.

Culture is not about making employees feel good. It is not about making employees happy. Culture is about performance. And, when employees feel valued and included, they are more likely to be engaged, motivated, and committed to the organization's success. Culture is a performance phenomenon. The work of culture is up to every person in the company. Culture is not a program. It is not an HR initiative. It is the sum of our collective behaviors and is an organizational initiative. The question becomes, "which behaviors work best for our team and will make us the best we can be?"

> *"The business of business is people."*
>
> *Herb Kelleher*

Southwest Airlines was not the only company to do this well. Here are some other stories of success to consider.

We the People Success Stories

The Zappos Way

Zappos, the online shoe and clothing retailer, is a shining example of a company that embodies the "We the People" philosophy. From its inception, Zappos has prioritized creating a culture where employees feel like family. CEO Tony Hsieh believed that satisfied employees lead to satisfied customers, which in turn leads to a successful business. Zappos has no traditional hierarchy, and every employee has a voice in shaping the company culture. Regular all-hands meetings, open communication channels, and a strong emphasis on core values ensure that everyone feels included and valued. This inclusive approach has resulted in high employee satisfaction, low turnover rates, and a fiercely loyal customer base.

Patagonia's Activism

Patagonia, the outdoor apparel company, has also built its success on a foundation of inclusivity and shared purpose. Patagonia's culture is deeply rooted in environmental activism and social responsibility. The company's founder, Yvon Chouinard, has always encouraged employees to be active participants in the company's mission to protect the planet. This shared sense of purpose unites employees and fosters a culture where everyone feels they are contributing to something meaningful. Patagonia empowers its employees to take initiative, voice their ideas, and participate in decision-making processes, ensuring that the company culture is a true reflection of its collective values.

Strategies for creating We the People

Creating a Culture of Inclusion

To cultivate a culture that embodies "We the People," leaders must take intentional steps to involve all employees in the cultural evolution of the company. Here are some strategies to consider:

1. **Open Communication:** Establish regular channels for open and honest communication. Encourage feedback and make it easy for employees to share their ideas and concerns.

2. **Empowerment:** Give employees the autonomy to make decisions and take ownership of their work. Empowerment leads to a sense of responsibility and investment in the company's success.

3. **Recognition:** Regularly acknowledge and celebrate the contributions of all employees. Recognition fosters a sense of belonging and motivates employees to continue giving their best.

4. **Inclusion:** Seek a diverse and inclusive workplace where different perspectives are valued. Diversity drives innovation and helps build a culture that reflects a wide range of experiences and ideas.

5. **Shared Values:** Define and communicate the company's core values clearly. Once you identify the core values, make sure you further define those values with associated behaviors that let employees know how to act in alignment with those values. (I outline this concept in detail in Chapter Three). Ensure these values and behaviors are modeled in everyday actions, are communicated regularly, and are instrumental in all decision-making processes.

We the People Exercises

Exercise: The Culture Canvas

To help leaders engage their employees in shaping the company culture, here is an exercise called the Culture Canvas:

1. **Gather Your Team:** Bring together a diverse group of employees from different departments and levels within the company. Make sure this team understands the changes they have the authority to make. (Include leadership in the team so changes can be made quickly and easily, if necessary.)

2. **Create the Canvas:** On a large piece of paper or a whiteboard, create the following sections:

    Culture:
    - How would we describe our current culture?
    - What is working well?
    - What would make us better if we changed?
    - What are we willing to do about it?

3. **Brainstorm and Collaborate:** Encourage everyone to contribute their ideas and experiences in each section of the canvas. Make sure all voices are heard and respected.

4. **Synthesize and Implement:** Review the contributions and identify common themes. Synthesize these into a cohesive framework that can be communicated and implemented across the organization.

5. **Review and Iterate:** Regularly revisit the Culture Canvas with your team to ensure it remains relevant and reflective of the evolving company culture.

We the People Summary

Building a company culture based on the principle of "We the People" requires a commitment to inclusion, collaboration, and shared responsibility. By valuing every employee's contribution and fostering an environment where everyone feels they belong, leaders can create a thriving, resilient, and successful organization. Remember, the true strength of a company lies in its people, and it is through their collective efforts that greatness is achieved.

In the next chapter, we will explore the concept of "a more perfect Union" and how striving for a proper culture fit between employee and organization propels a company toward excellence. Let's learn the practices and principles that help us better understand how our culture can serve to both attract and retain top talent.

CHAPTER 2

A More Perfect Union

The Art of Alignment

The phrase "a more perfect Union" from the Preamble to the Constitution signifies an ongoing journey toward improvement and unity. In the context of company culture, this concept highlights the importance of aligning individuals with the organization's values, mission, and vision. Achieving a "perfect union" within a company involves matching the right people to the culture, ensuring that every employee is not only a fit for the organization but also a contributor to its continued evolution and success.

The Importance of Cultural Fit

Cultural fit is more than just a buzzword; it's a critical factor in building a cohesive, productive, and resilient organization. When employees align with the company's culture, they are more likely to be engaged, motivated, and committed to their work. Conversely, a poor cultural fit can lead to dissatisfaction, disengagement, and high turnover rates. Identifying and hiring individuals who resonate with the company's values and vision is essential for fostering a harmonious, thriving, and productive workplace.

I am often perplexed, however, when I talk to leaders about finding employees who are a good culture fit. Few disagree on its importance, but few also understand and can describe their culture well enough to hire to it. If you want to attract people to your culture, you need to know exactly what your culture is and what you would like it to become. It is like thinking about you on your best day. What are the behaviors you exhibit on your best day? Similarly, what does your company or team look like on its best day? What are the behaviors you see from your team members? Those are what truly define your best culture.

Just west of Austin, Texas, a company called Texas Hill Country Provisions resides in a cool office constructed from an old train depot that was operational in Dumas, Texas during the 1930s. It was later shipped to Austin and houses Texas Hill Country Provisions today. This company sells Texas-themed apparel and products which represent their Hill Country roots. Every element of their office is curated to evoke a strong Texas feeling, from the products to the décor to the live music being played by Texas musicians in the headquarters. When hiring a new salesperson, one of the elements they look for is if someone can "vibe" with them. Even that language reflects their culture. Immediately, that word vibe will likely either attract you to the company or dissuade you from wanting to join. And that's the point! If you vibe well with the other employees, you will likely be a good match for the company and, therefore, enhance the culture. If you don't vibe well, you would likely not be attracted to work there or would be a bad hire if you did. A strong culture attracts the right fit and repels the wrong one.

When we understand what our culture is, we can then determine who we want to attract to become a part of it; to form a more perfect union between employee and organization. If this union is strong, we will get better performance. If the union is not a good fit, the performance will struggle.

> "Shaping your culture is more than half done when you hire your team."
>
> Jessica Herrin

A More Perfect Union Success Stories

Southwest Airlines' Hiring Philosophy

Southwest Airlines is renowned for its strong company culture, which prioritizes customer service, teamwork, and a fun-loving attitude. The airline's hiring philosophy centers on finding individuals who align with these cultural values. Rather than focusing solely on skills and experience, Southwest places a significant emphasis on attitude and personality. During the interview process, candidates are assessed for their cultural fit through behavioral questions and situational exercises.

If you have ever flown on Southwest Airlines, you might have noticed that one of their values is fun. They want to hire people with a good sense of humor. One of the interview questions they ask flight attendant candidates is, "Give me an example of a time when you used your sense of humor to diffuse a difficult situation." If the candidate does not have a good answer for this question, it indicates to the interviewer that this person is probably not a good culture fit, as the Southwest way is to bring humor and fun into the employee and customer experience. This approach ensures that new hires not only have the necessary skills but also embody the spirit of Southwest's culture, in this case, a sense of humor. As a result, Southwest has maintained high employee morale, low turnover rates, and exceptional customer satisfaction.

Netflix's Culture of Freedom and Responsibility

Netflix's culture is built on the principles of freedom and responsibility. The company believes in hiring individuals who are self-motivated, innovative, and aligned with its core values. Netflix's rigorous hiring process includes multiple rounds of interviews and cultural assessments to ensure that candidates are a good fit for the company's unique environment. By prioritizing cultural alignment, Netflix has created a workforce that thrives on autonomy and accountability. This cultural fit has been a key driver of Netflix's success, enabling the company to innovate rapidly and maintain its position as a leader in the entertainment industry. (Netflix is also renowned for its intolerance of "Brilliant Jerks." In other words, no matter how good you are at doing your job, if you are a jerk while doing it, you won't last at Netflix!)

Strategies for Achieving a Perfect Cultural Union

To create a more perfect union within your organization, consider the following strategies for aligning the right people with your company culture:

1. **Define Your Culture Clearly:** Clearly articulate your company's culture: not just what you are and what you do, but who you are when you do it. Make this specific in terms of the behaviors you want to see from your employees and leadership. Ensure those behaviors are communicated consistently across all levels of the organization.

2. **Assess Cultural Fit During Hiring:** Look beyond the resume. Develop a robust hiring process that includes cultural assessments and values alignment. Look for things like curiosity, integrity, and grit in the hire rather than simply looking at where someone was previously employed. Think about the type of person you want working with you as that is far more important than their previous employment. Use behavioral interview questions and situational exercises to evaluate candidates' alignment with your company's values and culture.

3. **Onboard with Culture in Mind:** Design an onboarding program that immerses new hires in your company culture. Provide opportunities for them to connect with colleagues, learn about the company's history and values, and understand their role in the broader mission. Remember how important stories are in this process. Tell the stories of your organization's creation, its struggles, its successes, and its vision. People remember and are attracted to stories.

4. **Foster Continuous Cultural Alignment:** Regularly revisit and reinforce your company's cultural values through training, team-building activities, and communication.

Encourage employees to contribute to the culture and provide feedback on how it can be improved. Communicate the values and behaviors as often as you can.

5. **Recognize and Reward Cultural Ambassadors:** Identify and celebrate employees who exemplify your company's culture. Recognize their behaviors and tie their success to them. Make your rewards and recognition reflective of your culture: if fun is part of who you are, reflect that in the recognition. There are no right or wrong values. There are only values that align and define your culture and those that do not. By knowing who your company is on its best day, you can identify those behaviors you want to reward and recognize.

Exercise: The Cultural Fit Workshop

To help leaders and teams align the right people with the company culture, here is an exercise called the Cultural Fit Workshop:

1. **Prepare the Workshop:** Invite a cross-functional group of employees, including representatives from HR, leadership, and hiring managers. Focus on inviting anyone who has interviewing responsibilities.

2. **Define Key Cultural Traits:** As a group, identify the key traits, behaviors, and values that define your company culture. Write these down on a whiteboard or flipchart. Think

specifically about the traits you want to see in a colleague. Be specific in defining what those traits look like in action.

3. **Create Interview Scenarios:** To assess candidates' alignment with core cultural traits, develop a set of behaviorally based interview questions and scenarios. (Behaviorally based interview questions focus on asking candidates to describe the behaviors they have demonstrated in the past around a particular trait.) Focus on having candidates describe their previous experiences, as past behavior is the best predictor of future behavior. For example, if teamwork is a core value, ask questions that require candidates to demonstrate their prior experience collaborating effectively. This will give you the best glimpse into how that candidate will behave when working for you.

4. **Role-Play Interviews:** Divide the participants into pairs or small groups and have them role-play interviews using the developed questions and scenarios. Each person should take turns being the interviewer and the interviewee. Ensure those people who interview candidates are trained in the interview process, especially in a behaviorally based interview model.

5. **Debrief and Refine:** After the role-play sessions, reconvene as a group to discuss the experience. What worked well? What could be improved? Refine the interview questions and scenarios based on the feedback.

6. **Implement and Monitor:** Integrate the refined interview questions into your hiring process. Monitor the outcomes

and adjust as needed to ensure they effectively identify candidates who are a good cultural fit.

A More Perfect Union Summary

Achieving a more perfect union with the people you bring into your company is an ongoing process that requires intentional effort and commitment. By focusing on cultural alignment and ensuring every employee resonates with the company's values and behaviors, leaders can build a cohesive, motivated, and high-performing workforce. A strong cultural fit not only enhances individual and organizational performance but also contributes to a positive and enduring company culture. Remember to look beyond the resume when hiring. Look for the traits you want to see in an employee, not just where the applicant has worked in the past.

In the next chapter, we will explore the concept of "establish Justice" and how your organization's values can be the differentiator to create a competitive advantage for your organization. Let's learn how the principles and practices will help integrate the values within your organization.

CHAPTER 3

Establish Justice

Defining Your Company's Value System

The phrase "establish Justice" in the Preamble to the Constitution underscores the vision of promoting fairness, equality, and ethical behavior in creating a just society. In the context of company culture, establishing justice means defining and embedding a value system that ensures fair treatment, transparency, and ethical conduct throughout the organization. In essence, we want to build an organization that instills fairness and trust.

The Role of Core Values

Core values are the fundamental beliefs that guide an organization's actions and decisions. They serve as a moral compass, shaping the behavior of employees and defining the company's identity. A well-defined value system not only helps to establish a fair and just workplace but also provides a framework for decision-making and conflict resolution. By aligning values with the company's mission and vision, leaders can create a cohesive and resilient culture that stands the test of time.

I estimate 80% of the companies I work with have some semblance of written values. The problem is an equal percentage of those companies do not have values they believe drive any kind of performance. I recently led a session with a group of leaders from different business sectors across the country. I asked by a show of hands how many of their organizations had written values. Almost every hand was raised. I asked them to keep their hands raised if they felt those values were a compelling driver of decision-making, hiring, and performance.

One hand remained raised out of a room of about 150 leaders.

When we define culture as a collection of the behaviors of the people within a team, group, or organization, it is important to tie those behaviors to your company's values. The values are your non-negotiables. The behaviors are the way we demonstrate those values. They are the embodiment of our culture. Our role as leaders is to provide the context or framework where those behaviors are communicated, rewarded, recognized, and supported. Conversely, if an employee chooses to behave outside of those behaviors, consequences will ensue.

Think about a football field. The sidelines represent "out of bounds," and the players clearly know if they step out of bounds, the play stops. In your organization, think about the sidelines being two key indicators of performance: finances and values. If you step out of the financial sideline, the play stops. That one is typically straightforward and easy to implement. It's the other sideline that is a little more difficult. If you step out of the values sideline, the play stops as well.

Employees who operate outside the organization's values are stealing your culture.

Your values should reflect your company on its best day and the behaviors are a description of how the employees behave on their best day.

> "Culture isn't just one aspect of the game; it is the game. In the end, an organization is nothing more than the collective capacity of its people to create value."
>
> Louis Gerstner

Establish Justice Success Stories

Ben & Jerry's Commitment to Social Justice

Ben & Jerry's, the iconic ice cream company, is renowned for its commitment to social justice and ethical practices. From its inception, the company has embedded values of fairness, equality, and environmental responsibility into its business model. Ben & Jerry's mission statement emphasizes the importance of producing high-quality products, achieving sustainable financial growth, and advancing social causes. The company's core values are reflected in its sourcing practices, labor policies, and advocacy efforts. By staying true to its values, Ben & Jerry's has built a loyal customer base and a reputation for integrity and social responsibility.

The Honest Company's Transparency

The Honest Company, co-founded by actress Jessica Alba, was established with a mission to provide safe, eco-friendly products for families. Transparency, honesty, and sustainability are at the heart of the company's values. The Honest Company is committed to providing clear information about its products' ingredients and manufacturing processes, ensuring that customers can make informed choices. This commitment to transparency has earned the company trust and loyalty from consumers who value ethical and environmentally responsible practices. By establishing a value system centered on honesty and integrity, The Honest Company has differentiated itself in a competitive market.

Strategies to Identifying and Defining Core Values

To establish a value system that promotes justice and fair treatment, leaders must take deliberate steps to identify and define the core values that will shape their company's culture. Here are some strategies to consider:

1. **Engage Stakeholders:** Involve employees, leaders, and other stakeholders in the process of identifying core values. Conduct surveys, focus groups, and discussions to gather diverse perspectives and insights.

2. **Reflect on the Mission and Vision:** Ensure the core values align with the company's mission and vision. The values should support the organization's purpose and long-term goals.

3. **Prioritize Fairness and Ethical Behavior:** Emphasize values that promote fairness, transparency, and ethical conduct. These principles are essential for building trust and integrity within the organization.

4. **Differentiate Your Organization:** Think about what makes your organization unique. This is the opportunity to differentiate your organization from your competition. A good differentiating value can help attract the right candidates and customers.

5. **Be Specific and Actionable:** Define values in clear and specific terms. Avoid vague or generic statements. Ensure the values are actionable and can be integrated into daily practices and decision-making processes. Think about being able to hire, promote, reward, recognize, and even fire to the values.

6. **Communicate and Reinforce:** Clearly communicate the core values to all employees. Reinforce these values through training, policies, and regular communication. Celebrate and recognize behaviors that exemplify the values.

Exercise: The Values Workshop

To help leaders and teams establish a value system that defines their company culture, here is an exercise called the Values Workshop:

1. **Gather Your Team:** Assemble a diverse group of employees from different departments and levels within the company. This activity can be conducted in person (preferred) or remotely.

2. **Brainstorm Values:** Divide the participants into small groups and ask each group to brainstorm a list of values they believe are important for the company. Encourage them to think about values that represent who the company is on its best day. Try not to succumb to the lowest common denominator values. Think about your strategic advantage in the marketplace, and consider what will also promote fairness, transparency, and ethical behavior into the future. If your company values are already written, consider a similar exercise to validate those values in today's climate. If you find your current values are strong, relevant, and will take your organization to the next level, the exercise of validating those values is a worthwhile practice.

3. **Consolidate and Prioritize:** Reconvene as a whole group and consolidate the lists of values. Discuss each value and prioritize those that resonate most with the company's mission and vision. Aim to identify no more than 5-7 core values.

4. **Define Each Value:** For each core value, work together to create a clear and specific definition. Describe what that value means in the context of your work environment. A value such as integrity can have different meanings in different contexts. Make sure you are clear, so you

employees have an accurate picture of the company expectation around that value.

5. **Write Behavior Statements for Each Value:** Create 3 – 5 behavior statements for each value. Think about behaviors that will help employees see a pathway to success. Many behaviors sound like a slogan or cheer. For example, a behavioral description of teamwork, defined as "We are one team," doesn't provide specific actions for the employee. The behavior statements should specifically describe what that value looks like when it happens in your organization. Different departments might need to write their own, specific behaviors as well, but it is important to have one, overarching set of behaviors that can apply to all.

6. **Implement and Monitor:** Integrate the core values into company policies, training programs, and performance evaluations. Regularly monitor and review the values to ensure they remain relevant and impactful. Review behaviors regularly to validate them and confirm they are relevant and driving performance. Look at companies like The Culture Think Tank (www.theculturethinktank.com) that offer an easy, 5-question Culture Snapshot to keep your finger on the pulse of your culture.

BB's Tex-Orleans, a Cajun restaurant chain in Houston and San Antonio, exemplifies strong company values and behaviors. Rooted in Cajun traditions passed down from the owner's grandmother, known as "Maw-Maw," their menu reflects authentic flavors from her original kitchen. One of their core values, "Our Roux is our Krewe," emphasizes the importance of their foundation: their people. If you aren't from Louisiana, that value is the equivalent of "Our foundation is our people." Key behaviors include: "When you screw up, say you did and learn from it;" and, "Laugh at yourself; accept imperfections." Those colorful behaviors give employees a good understanding of the culture at BB's.

Establish Justice Summary

Establishing justice within your company involves creating a value system that promotes the best of what your organization can be, including fairness, transparency, and ethical behavior. By identifying and defining core values that align with your company's mission and vision, you can foster a culture of integrity and trust. Values also serve as a template for the behaviors you want to see from your employees daily. Remember, a strong value system not only guides behavior and decision-making but also serves as the foundation for a just and equitable workplace.

In the next chapter, we will explore the concept of "ensure domestic Tranquility" and how fostering a positive and supportive work environment can enhance employee well-being and organizational success. Let's learn the practices and strategies that promote justice and tranquility within the workplace.

CHAPTER 4

Ensure Domestic Tranquility

Fostering a Positive Work Environment

The phrase "ensure domestic Tranquility" from the Preamble to the Constitution speaks to the importance of peace and harmony within a community. In the business world, this describes leadership's role in creating a safe environment where employees can do their best work. It does not mean we are chasing employee happiness, but we know that employees who feel safe, supported, heard, and challenged behave better than those who feel unsupported and unsafe. Happiness is the employees' choice. Our role is to ensure we create a work environment where employees are safe, supported, challenged, and encouraged.

This concept emphasizes the need for a supportive and engaging work environment that promotes employee well-being. This does not mean we don't work hard and aren't driving performance and results. Again, the purpose of a strong culture is to promote strong organizational results. When we can create a supportive environment that drives results, we can attract and retain top talent and be competitive in our marketplace. This chapter will explore the strategies and practices that leaders can implement to ensure domestic tranquility and promote employee well-being.

The Importance of Employee Well-Being

A recent Gallup Poll reported only 33% of employees are "thriving" in their feeling of well-being. Factors that affect well-being include health, job satisfaction, stress levels, and work-life balance. Imagine the increase in performance if we could flip that number to only 33% of employees who felt like they weren't thriving. Our companies would be transformed. The good news is we can have an impact on those factors affecting our employees' well-being.

Employee well-being encompasses physical, mental, and emotional health. The Pandemic of 2020 illuminated the need for people to feel safe. When the world shut down, there was a rise in anxiety, depression, frustration, and isolation. The World Health Organization (WHO) reported that anxiety and depression increased by 25% among adults during the first year of the Pandemic and called on countries to increase mental health services and support.

This event caused leaders to better understand how an employee's well-being has a direct effect on that employee's performance. Conversely, when employees feel supported and valued, they are more likely to be engaged, motivated, and productive. A stressful and unsupportive work environment can lead to burnout, high turnover rates, and decreased performance. Promoting employee well-being is not just a moral imperative; it is also a strategic advantage that can drive organizational success.

> *"Few things can paralyze the progress of any team or organization like anxiety."*
>
> *Chester Elton*

Ensure Domestic Tranquility Success Stories Google's Comprehensive Well-Being Programs

Google is well-known for its commitment to employee well-being. The company offers a wide range of programs and benefits designed to support the physical, mental, and emotional health of its employees. These include on-site fitness centers, healthy meal options, flexible work hours, and mental health resources such as counseling and mindfulness programs. Google also fosters a culture of inclusivity and support through initiatives like employee resource groups and diversity training. By prioritizing well-being, Google has created a positive and productive work environment that attracts and retains top talent.

Salesforce's Ohana Culture

Salesforce has built its success on a culture of well-being and support known as the "Ohana Culture." Inspired by the Hawaiian concept of family, this culture emphasizes the importance of community, collaboration, and mutual support. Salesforce provides employees with a variety of well-being initiatives, including generous parental leave, volunteer time off, and wellness reimbursements.

The company also promotes mental health awareness and provides resources such as Employee Assistance Programs (EAPs) and mindfulness training. Salesforce's commitment to well-being has resulted in high employee satisfaction, strong retention rates, and a sense of belonging among its workforce.

Strategies for Promoting Employee Well-Being

To create a safe and supportive work environment, leaders must implement strategies that prioritize the well-being of their employees. Here are some key practices to consider:

1. **Support Work-Life Balance:** Be willing to consider flexible work arrangements, such as remote work, flexible hours, and paid time off. More than 73% of polled workers say work-life balance is a key factor when choosing a job, second only to salary. If we support employees in managing their work-life balance, it can reduce stress and help prevent burnout. It's also helpful to remind employees that work-life balance doesn't always happen daily or weekly. Encourage them to see the longer game in terms of seasonality of work: some weeks/months are busy when perhaps others aren't. Consider striking the work-life balance over a longer period than daily or weekly.

2. **Provide Mental Health Resources:** Offer access to mental health resources, such as counseling services, EAPs, and mindfulness programs. Promote mental health awareness

and create a stigma-free environment where employees feel comfortable seeking help.

3. **Encourage Physical Health:** Provide opportunities for physical activity, such as on-site fitness centers, gym memberships, or wellness programs. Promote healthy eating by offering nutritious meal options and snacks.

4. **Foster a Positive Culture:** Create a culture of inclusivity, support, and collaboration. Encourage open communication, recognize and celebrate achievements, and provide opportunities for team-building and social connection.

5. **Offer Professional Development:** Support employees' professional growth by providing opportunities for training, development, and career advancement. Encourage continuous learning and skill-building to help employees feel fulfilled and motivated.

6. **Create a Safe Work Environment:** Ensure the physical work environment is safe and conducive to well-being. Address issues such as ergonomics, air quality, and noise levels to create a comfortable and healthy workspace to create physical safety. Psychological safety is also critical to a thriving culture. Ensure employees can voice any issues and that leaders are trained in how to deal with issues like stress management, anxiety, and a sense of overwhelm. Don't allow behaviors like bullying, aggression, or discrimination to reside in your culture.

Exercise: The Well-Being Assessment

To help leaders and teams assess and improve their workplace well-being initiatives, here is an exercise called the Well-Being Assessment:

1. **Gather Input:** Create a well-being survey to gather employee feedback on their current well-being and identify areas for improvement. (A copyright-free sample is available at the end of this book). The survey can be informal or formal, but it should cover aspects such as work-life balance, mental health, physical health, and overall job satisfaction.

2. **Analyze Results:** Analyze the survey results to identify common themes and areas where employees feel supported or where they experience challenges. Look for patterns and trends that can inform your well-being initiatives.

3. **Develop Action Plans:** Based on the survey findings, develop action plans to address the identified areas for improvement. Involve employees in the planning process to ensure that the initiatives meet their needs and preferences.

4. **Implement Initiatives:** Don't administer any survey if you are not willing to make some changes! Roll out the well-being initiatives, ensuring clear communication and accessibility for all employees. Provide training and

resources as needed to support the implementation. These initiatives can be good recruiting tactics, so make sure to communicate them during interviews.

5. **Monitor and Adjust:** Regularly monitor the impact of the well-being initiatives through follow-up surveys, feedback sessions, and performance metrics. Adjust the initiatives as needed to ensure they continue to meet the evolving needs of employees.

Ensure Domestic Tranquility Summary:

Promoting employee well-being and ensuring a safe and engaging workplace is essential for creating a positive and productive environment. By implementing strategies that support physical, mental, and emotional health, leaders can foster a culture of well-being that enhances employee satisfaction and organizational success. Remember, a safe and supportive work environment not only benefits employees but also drives long-term business performance.

In the next chapter, we will explore the concept of "provide for the common Defense" and how leaders can build resilient teams and systems to protect the organization from internal and external challenges. Let's learn how to implement the principles and practices that promote organizational resilience and stability.

CHAPTER 5

Provide for the Common Defense

Building Resilient Teams and Systems

The phrase "provide for the common Defense" from the Preamble to the Constitution highlights the importance of protecting and safeguarding a community or nation from external threats. In the corporate world, this concept extends to building resilient teams and systems that can withstand both external competition and internal challenges. Understanding your competition, whether it comes from outside the organization or from within, is crucial for maintaining a strong and stable company, and is a primary role in leadership. This chapter will explore strategies for defending against these threats and fostering a resilient, competitive organization.

The Dual Nature of Competition

Competition in business is not limited to rival companies striving for market share. Internal competition, such as conflicting priorities, inefficient processes, and siloed departments, can also undermine an organization's success. Leaders must recognize and address both external and internal competitive pressures to ensure the organization remains resilient and cohesive.

When working for Southwest Airlines, Herb Kelleher had an uncanny way of creating an enemy when it appeared we had become complacent. He would often come into the Southwest Airlines' University for People where I worked and tell us of threats on the West Coast from America West Airlines or from other carriers. He would challenge us to get our people focused so big, bad America West wouldn't take over our market share. (America West merged with US Airways in 2007 which then merged with American Airlines in 2015.) In reality, Herb wasn't nearly as concerned with America West stealing market share as he was with the internal threat of employees being complacent. Instead of taking complacency on directly, he dismissed it by engaging our own competitive spirit which eliminated any complacency we may have had.

Assessing external threats, whether real or perceived, as well as assessing internal threats is critical for leadership. And don't underestimate the power of the knowledge of your frontline employees in this endeavor. Your employees are living the processes that leadership creates. They are often the first to see the unintended consequences of those processes. Ask for their opinions and their feedback. That exchange will not only help you unearth internal and external threats, but it can also help support a trusting environment.

> "When there is no enemy within, the enemies outside cannot hurt you."
>
> *Winston Churchill*

Provide for the Common Defense Success Stories

IBM's Adaptability and Innovation

IBM, one of the oldest and most respected technology companies, has demonstrated remarkable resilience and adaptability over the years. Faced with intense external competition from other tech giants and startups, IBM has continuously evolved its business model and product offerings. The company recognized the need to innovate and diversify, shifting from hardware to software and services, and investing heavily in emerging technologies such as artificial intelligence and cloud computing. Internally, IBM fostered a culture of collaboration and continuous improvement, breaking down silos and encouraging cross-functional teams to work together. This adaptability and focus on innovation have allowed IBM to remain a competitive force in the industry.

Toyota's Continuous Improvement Philosophy

Toyota's success is built on its commitment to the principle of Kaizen, or continuous improvement. This philosophy encourages all employees to contribute to improving processes, reducing waste, and enhancing quality. By fostering a culture of continuous improvement, Toyota has been able to identify and address internal inefficiencies, making the company more resilient to external competition. Additionally, Toyota's focus on teamwork and collaboration has helped to eliminate internal competition and align all employees toward common goals. This holistic approach to competition and improvement has made Toyota a leader in the automotive industry.

Strategies for Defending Against Competition

To provide for the common defense of the organization, leaders must implement strategies that address both external and internal competitive pressures. Here are some key practices to consider:

1. **Understand the Landscape:** Conduct regular market analyses to understand the competitive landscape. Identify key competitors, analyze their strengths and weaknesses, and assess how your organization can differentiate itself. Be willing to look internally as sometimes our biggest enemies are those within.

2. **Foster a Culture of Collaboration:** Make sure the values and behaviors you created include language around collaboration and working as a team. Break down silos and encourage cross-functional collaboration. Make sure your culture allows for mistakes to be discussed openly. Mistakes made for the first time can be informative. Create a culture where fear doesn't win the battle over creativity.

3. **Invest in Innovation:** Allocate resources for research and development to stay ahead of industry trends. Encourage employees to think creatively and propose innovative ideas that can drive the business forward.

4. **Streamline Internal Processes:** Identify and eliminate inefficiencies within internal processes. Implement continuous improvement methodologies, such as Lean or Six Sigma, to enhance productivity and reduce waste.

5. **Build Resilient Teams:** Develop teams that are adaptable, skilled, and capable of handling challenges. Teams that support teams can be a more inclusive and practical model than traditional top-down management. Provide training and development opportunities to ensure employees have the necessary skills and knowledge to thrive in a competitive environment.

6. **Enhance Communication:** Employees want more communication than leaders are often able to provide. If you maintain open lines of communication throughout the organization, this allows employees to be and feel heard and allows leadership to understand the issues in real time. Ensure employees are informed about strategic goals, competitive threats, and internal changes. Transparency fosters trust and alignment.

Exercise: The SWOT Analysis Workshop

To help leaders and teams assess and address both external and internal competition, here is an exercise called the SWOT Analysis Workshop:

1. **Gather Your Team:** Assemble a diverse group of employees from different departments and levels within the company. This exercise can be conducted in person or remotely.

2. **Introduce SWOT Analysis:** Explain the concept of SWOT analysis, which involves identifying the organization›s

Strengths, Weaknesses, Opportunities, and Threats. This can be applied to your company as a whole or to an individual department.

3. **Conduct the Analysis:** Divide the participants into small groups and assign each group one of the SWOT categories. Ask them to brainstorm and list the key points for their assigned category. For example:

   - **Strengths:** What are our internal strengths? What do we do well?
   - **Weaknesses:** What are our internal weaknesses? Where can we improve?
   - **Opportunities:** What external opportunities can we capitalize on?
   - **Threats:** What external threats do we face? How can we mitigate them?

4. **Share and Consolidate:** Reconvene as a whole group and have each small group share their findings. Consolidate the lists and discuss the key points.

5. **Develop Action Plans:** Based on the SWOT analysis, develop action plans to leverage strengths, address weaknesses, seize opportunities, and mitigate threats. Assign responsibilities and set timelines for implementation.

6. **Monitor and Adjust:** Regularly review the progress of the action plans and adjust them as needed. Continuously monitor the competitive landscape and internal processes to ensure the organization remains resilient and competitive.

Provide for the Common Defense Summary:

Providing for the common defense of your organization involves understanding and addressing both external and internal competitive pressures. By fostering a culture of collaboration, investing in innovation, streamlining processes, and building resilient teams, leaders can create a strong and stable company capable of withstanding challenges. Remember, a resilient organization not only defends against competition but also thrives in a dynamic and competitive environment.

In the next chapter, we will explore the concept of "promote the general Welfare" and how leaders can create a supportive and thriving community within the workplace. The next step is to better understand the principles and practices that enhance employee well-being and contribute to overall organizational success.

CHAPTER 6

Promote the General Welfare

Creating a Thriving Workplace and Being a Good Neighbor

The phrase "promote the general Welfare" from the Preamble to the Constitution underscores the responsibility to foster well-being and prosperity within the community. In the corporate context, this extends beyond creating a healthy workplace to include being a good neighbor and contributing positively to the broader community. This chapter will explore strategies for promoting the general welfare within the organization and its surrounding community, emphasizing the dual role of fostering employee well-being, and engaging in corporate social responsibility.

The Interconnectedness of Workplace and Community

A thriving workplace and a supportive community are interdependent. Employees who feel supported and valued at work are more likely to engage positively with their communities, and companies that contribute to their communities can enhance their reputation, attract talent, and build stronger stakeholder relationships. By promoting the general welfare, companies can create a positive feedback loop that benefits both their workforce and the broader society. This is not just a neighborly thing to do, it is also a strategic advantage in the marketplace. A 2024 study by America's Charities reported 71% of surveyed employees say it is imperative or very important to work where culture is supportive of giving and volunteering. Those organizations with strong cultures that help our world are more likely to hire the best candidates. Similarly, consumers are looking for products and services that provide for the general welfare and often choose away from those that do not.

Wegmans Food Markets is a privately held supermarket chain headquartered in Gates, New York. It was founded in 1916 and now has over 109 stores in more than eight states. The allure of Wegmans is not just in the quality and pricing of the products they sell, but its success rests in how they give back to their communities. Their tagline of, "Together, we can improve lives and make neighborhoods stronger" is personified in their scholarship programs, assistance to the elderly, and promoting the underserved population in their communities. Wegmans is about far more than selling groceries. They are about building sustainable communities. It is the essence of who they are and simultaneously serves as their compelling market advantage.

> "There could be no definition of a successful life that does not include service to others."
>
> *President George H. W. Bush*

Promote the General Welfare Success Stories

Patagonia's Commitment to Environmental Stewardship

Patagonia, the outdoor clothing company, is a prime example of a business that prioritizes both internal well-being and external community engagement. Internally, Patagonia fosters a healthy workplace by offering flexible work schedules, on-site childcare, and wellness programs. Externally, the company is deeply committed to environmental sustainability. Patagonia donates 1% of its sales to environmental causes, encourages employees to volunteer for environmental initiatives, and advocates for policies that protect natural resources. This dual focus on employee well-being and community engagement has built Patagonia's reputation as a socially responsible company and strengthened its connection with environmentally conscious consumers.

Salesforce's 1-1-1 Philanthropic Model

Salesforce's 1-1-1 model dedicates 1% of the company's equity, 1% of its product, and 1% of employees' time to philanthropic efforts. This model has enabled Salesforce to support numerous charitable initiatives and community projects. Internally, Salesforce promotes employee well-being through comprehensive health benefits, wellness programs, and a culture of inclusivity. By integrating philanthropy into its business model, Salesforce not only enhances its community impact but also fosters a sense of purpose and pride among its employees. This commitment to the general welfare has strengthened Salesforce's brand and deepened its ties with the community.

Strategies for Promoting the General Welfare
To promote the general welfare, leaders must implement strategies that enhance employee well-being and contribute positively to the community. Here are some key practices to consider:

1. **Support Employee Well-Being:** Invest in comprehensive health and wellness programs for employees, including mental health resources, fitness initiatives, and flexible work arrangements. The Pandemic of 2020 ushered in the new era of remote work, which many employees enjoy. While every job is different and some may not have a remote component available, leaders who are willing to listen to the needs of employees enjoy better employee engagement and lower overall turnover. If you foster a supportive and inclusive work environment that values employee well-being, employees are more willing to give back to the company and to their communities in meaningful ways.

2. **Engage in Corporate Social Responsibility:** Develop and implement CSR initiatives that align with the company's values and mission. This could include charitable donations, volunteer programs, and sustainability efforts. Create a CSR team that encourages employees to get involved in their communities. Remember to promote those initiatives in the community. This helps attract potential employees who could be a good culture fit.

3. **Encourage Employee Volunteerism:** Provide opportunities and incentives for employees to volunteer in their communities. Offer paid volunteer time off and support employee-led community projects

4. **Partner with Local Organizations:** Collaborate with local nonprofits, schools, and community groups to address pressing community needs. Establish partnerships that leverage the company's resources and expertise for positive impact.

5. **Promote Sustainability:** Implement sustainable business practices that reduce the company's environmental footprint. Encourage employees to adopt eco-friendly habits and support environmental initiatives.

6. **Foster a Culture of Giving:** Cultivate a culture that values giving back to the community. Recognize and celebrate employees' contributions to community service and philanthropic efforts. If this is an important part of your company culture, make sure it is reflected in your values and behaviors as that will allow the culture of giving to continue regardless of any changes in leadership.

Exercise: The Community Impact Workshop

To help leaders and teams develop and implement strategies for promoting the general welfare, here is an exercise called the Community Impact Workshop:

1. **Assemble a Diverse Team:** Gather employees from various departments and levels within the company who are passionate about community engagement and employee well-being. Again, this is a great exercise whether employees are in person or remote.

2. **Identify Community Needs**: Conduct research to identify key needs and challenges within the local community. Engage with local organizations, community leaders, and residents to gain insights. This does not need to be a formal process; it can consist of round table discussions, town hall meetings, or just conversations with customers, community members and community leaders. It is important to know how we can be good corporate citizens.

3. **Brainstorm Initiatives:** Divide participants into small groups and ask each group to brainstorm potential initiatives that address the identified community needs and promote employee well-being. Encourage creativity and innovation.

4. **Prioritize and Plan:** Reconvene as a whole group and prioritize the most impactful and feasible initiatives. Develop action plans for each initiative, including goals, timelines, resources, and responsible parties.

5. **Implement and Monitor:** Launch the initiatives and watch their progress. Collect feedback from employees and community members to assess the impact and adjust as needed.

6. **Celebrate and Share:** Recognize and celebrate the contributions of employees and the positive impact on the community. Share success stories internally and externally to inspire continued engagement and support. This exercise is a great recruiting opportunity to engage our top talent!

Promote the General Welfare Summary

Promoting the general welfare involves creating a healthy workplace and being a good neighbor in the community. By supporting employee well-being and engaging in corporate social responsibility, leaders can foster a positive and thriving environment both within the organization and in the broader community. Remember, a commitment to the general welfare not only enhances the company's reputation and stakeholder relationships but also contributes to a more just and prosperous society.

In the next chapter, we will explore the concept of "secure the Blessings of Liberty" and how leaders can empower employees and foster a culture of autonomy, creativity, and innovation. As our culture becomes more mature, we want to learn the principles and practices that promote individual and organizational freedom and success now and for the future.

CHAPTER 7

Secure the Blessings of Liberty

Empowering Employees and Fostering a Culture of Autonomy

The phrase "secure the Blessings of Liberty" from the Preamble to the Constitution is both powerful and beautiful. It emphasizes the importance of preserving freedom and opportunities for future generations. In the context of a business, this concept translates to empowering employees, fostering a culture of autonomy, and promoting creativity and innovation. When employees are given the liberty to explore, innovate, and take ownership of their work, it leads to a more dynamic, engaged, and productive workforce. This chapter will explore strategies for securing the blessings of liberty within your organization.

The Strength of Empowerment

Empowering employees means giving them the authority, resources, and support they need to make decisions and take action.

Empowered employees are more likely to feel valued, motivated, and committed to the organization's success. The statistics on the strength of empowerment at work include that when empowerment is high, 67% of employees are willing to put in extra effort, compared to only 4% when empowerment is low. Empowerment also helps employees respond to challenges, find opportunities for improvement, and drive innovation. By fostering a culture of autonomy and trust, leaders can unlock the full potential of their workforce.

My work gives me the opportunity to travel to visit clients and experience their cultures first-hand. On a recent trip to Chicago, I visited a Pret-a-Manger store to grab lunch and witness the culture of Pret. Pret-a-Manger is a British sandwich and coffee shop headquartered in London, England. They run an open-door policy where there are no offices and all leadership, including the CEO, is always approachable. (Keep in mind, this is a multi-national organization with a combined 697 stores in the US and twelve other countries). Employees across their enterprise are encouraged and invited to have a voice and are afforded many opportunities to share their voices in staff meetings, team briefs and regular meetings with leadership. And Pret knows how to hire.

Their staff are not selected based on their experience making sandwiches or brewing coffee. The Pret-a-Manger interviewers look for three things in their hiring: Passion, Clarity, and Teamwork. If the candidate is selected for hire, they are invited to attend Pret Academy where they are taught not only how to do the functions of their job, but they are immersed in the Pret culture which is about many things including empowerment. Team members have the autonomy to give a free drink to a customer to spread the "Joy of Pret." They do not need approval. They are empowered to spread joy to their customers. Leadership trusts them to know when and how to make that decision.

> *"If your actions create a legacy that inspires others to dream more, learn more, do more and become more, then you are an excellent leader."*
>
> Dolly Parton

Secure the Blessings of Liberty Success Stories

Netflix's Culture of Freedom and Responsibility

Netflix is renowned for its unique corporate culture that emphasizes freedom and responsibility. The company trusts its employees to make decisions and encourages them to take risks and innovate. Netflix's culture is built on the belief that the best work comes from individuals who are free to act and are held accountable for their results. This approach has led to a highly engaged and creative workforce, capable of driving the company's success in the competitive entertainment industry. By securing the blessings of liberty, Netflix has fostered a culture of continuous innovation and excellence.

3M's 15% Rule

3M, a global innovation company, has long championed employee empowerment through its famous 15% rule. This policy allows employees to spend 15% of their work time on projects and ideas of their choosing, regardless of their direct job responsibilities. This freedom has led to the development of numerous successful products, including the Post-it Note. By giving employees the liberty to explore their interests and experiment with new ideas, 3M has cultivated a culture of creativity and innovation that drives its growth and success.

Strategies for Empowering Employees

To secure the blessings of liberty within your organization, leaders must implement strategies that empower employees and foster a culture of autonomy. Here are some key practices to consider:

1. **Trust and Delegate:** Trust employees to make decisions and delegate responsibilities accordingly. Avoid micromanaging and give employees the freedom to take ownership of their work. Trust does not coexist well with fear. One of the quickest ways to work on building trust in your organization is to start by removing fear. When employees feel fear, they lose the desire to create, to be bold, and to try new things. It takes an environment of trust to make those things happen.

2. **Provide Resources and Support:** Ensure employees have the resources, tools, and support they need to succeed. Invest in training and development to help them build the skills and knowledge needed for their roles.

3. **Encourage Risk-Taking and Innovation:** Create an environment where employees feel safe to take risks and propose innovative ideas. Celebrate successes and learn from failures, fostering a culture of continuous improvement and innovation.

4. **Promote Open Communication:** Maintain open lines of communication and encourage feedback and ideas from all levels of the organization. Ensure employees feel heard and valued.

5. **Recognize and Reward Contributions:** Acknowledge and reward employees for their contributions and achievements. Recognize both individual and team accomplishments to reinforce a culture of collaboration and mutual respect.

6. **Foster a Growth Mindset:** Encourage a growth mindset by promoting continuous learning and development. The opposite of a growth mindset is a closed one. Help employees keep a growth mindset by providing opportunities for employees to pursue their interests and expand their skill sets.

Exercise: The Empowerment Audit

To help leaders and teams assess and enhance their strategies for employee empowerment, here is an exercise called the Empowerment Audit:

1. **Gather Your Team:** Assemble a diverse group of employees from different departments and levels within the company. Remember to choose different people (if possible) for each of these exercises so all employees feel included.

2. **Assess Current Practices:** Conduct a thorough assessment of current empowerment practices. (A copy-right free sample Assessment is available at the end of this book.) Discuss how decisions are made, how responsibilities are delegated, and how employees are supported in their roles.

3. **Identify Barriers:** Identify any barriers to empowerment within the organization. These could include lack of trust, insufficient resources, or restrictive policies and procedures.

4. **Brainstorm Solutions:** Divide participants into small groups and ask each group to brainstorm potential solutions to the identified barriers. Encourage creative thinking and innovative ideas.

5. **Develop Action Plans:** Reconvene as a whole group and prioritize the most impactful and possible solutions. Develop action plans to implement these solutions, including goals, timelines, resources, and responsible parties.

6. **Monitor and Adjust:** Regularly review the progress of the action plans and make adjustments as needed. Continuously seek feedback from employees to ensure that empowerment practices are effective and aligned with their needs.

Secure the Blessings of Liberty Summary

Securing the blessings of liberty within your organization involves empowering employees and fostering a culture of autonomy, creativity, and innovation. By trusting employees, providing resources and support, encouraging risk-taking, and promoting open communication, leaders can create an environment where individuals feel valued and motivated to contribute their best work. Remember, a culture of empowerment not only enhances employee satisfaction and engagement but also drives organizational success and resilience.

In the next chapter, we will explore the concept of "to ourselves and our Posterity" and how leaders can build a sustainable and enduring legacy for future generations. Understanding and implementing the principles and practices that ensure long-term success will positively affect both the organization and the wider community.

CHAPTER 8

To Ourselves and Our Posterity

Building a Sustainable and Enduring Legacy

The phrase "to ourselves and our Posterity" from the Preamble to the Constitution underscores the importance of creating a lasting impact for current and future generations. In the context of a business, this means building a sustainable and enduring legacy that benefits employees, stakeholders, and the wider community both now and in the future. Not only do we want our organizations to last beyond the current leadership, but we also want the culture of the organization to last beyond the current leadership. By ensuring the values, behaviors, and practices in earlier chapters, we are building a culture that will last. We want our cultures to be so specifically defined and systematized within the organization that if there is a change in leadership, we recruit a new leader to our culture rather than worrying about losing our culture to a new leader. This chapter will explore strategies for ensuring long-term success and positive impact, focusing on sustainability, corporate social responsibility, and forward-thinking leadership.

The Importance of a Sustainable Legacy

A sustainable legacy is about more than just financial success; it encompasses environmental stewardship, social responsibility, community impact, and ethical governance. Companies that prioritize sustainability and long-term impact are better positioned to navigate challenges, attract and retain talent, and build strong relationships with stakeholders. By thinking beyond immediate profits and considering the broader implications of their actions, leaders can create a legacy that endures and inspires future generations.

Over the next decade, an estimated 5 million companies holding over $10 trillion in assets will change ownership. However, only 20 to 30% of those businesses will sell, and few will meet their asking price. To preserve and enhance value, it is crucial to strengthen both the operational processes and the successful employee and leadership behaviors that define the organization's culture.

During my time of leadership at Southwest Airlines, we had a vexing problem. Herb Kelleher, then President and CEO, was credited for much of the success of the culture at Southwest. And Wall Street knew it. The fear was that when Herb retired, the culture would leave with him. And, they had a point. In a cult-of-personality culture, this can happen. Oftentimes, dynamic leaders do not systematize their own uniqueness to the company and its culture, therefore leaving the culture vulnerable upon the leader's departure.

One of the ways we thwarted this at Southwest was through systems. We built systems that integrated the company's values and behaviors and thus imprinted Herb's uniqueness into the culture indefinitely. We ensured throughout the lifecycle of both the employee and the customer that the values would be preserved and experienced by all. We systematized fun in our interviews by having flight attendant candidates sing songs or perform a skit as part of the interview. Once hired, we encouraged flight attendants to bring their personalities into their work by creatively delivering the safety announcements and having fun with passengers. We created processes to celebrate and engage customers by playing games in the gate areas and on the aircraft. We built the systems that were designed to allow employees to have fun. Southwest, after all, is the LUV airline. We ensured the values were not only understood, but they were integrated throughout the company's processes. In essence, Herb lives on at Southwest Airlines even after he left.

> *"Too old to plant trees for my own gratification. I shall do it for my posterity."*
>
> *Thomas Jefferson*

To Ourselves and our Posterity Success Stories

Unilever's Sustainable Living Plan
Unilever, a global consumer goods company, has long been a leader in sustainability and corporate social responsibility. In 2010, the company launched the Unilever Sustainable Living Plan, which aimed to decouple business growth from environmental impact while increasing positive social impact. The plan set ambitious goals across areas such as health and well-being, environmental sustainability, and enhanced livelihoods. By integrating

sustainability into its core business strategy, Unilever has reduced its environmental footprint, improved social outcomes, and driven long-term growth. This commitment to sustainability has not only benefited the planet and society but has also strengthened Unilever's brand and market position.

Interface's Mission Zero

Interface, a leading modular flooring manufacturer, embarked on a mission in 1994 to become the world's first environmentally sustainable and restorative company. Known as Mission Zero, this ambitious goal aimed to eliminate any negative impact the company might have on the environment by 2020. Interface focused on reducing waste, using renewable energy, and redesigning products to be more sustainable. Through innovation and dedication, Interface achieved considerable progress toward its Mission Zero goals, setting a powerful example for other companies. By prioritizing sustainability, Interface not only contributed to environmental conservation but also built a resilient and forward-thinking business.

Strategies for Building a Sustainable Legacy

To build a sustainable and enduring legacy, leaders must implement strategies that prioritize long-term impact and responsible practices. Here are some key practices to consider:

1. **Adopt a Long-Term Vision:** Develop a clear and compelling vision for the future that emphasizes the best elements of your products or services and the culture

to live indefinitely. Identify those traits that define your competitive advantage in the marketplace and integrate them into everything you do. Communicate this vision to all stakeholders and align organizational strategies accordingly.

2. **Integrate Sustainability into Business Strategy:** Incorporate behavioral sustainability into the core business strategy and decision-making processes. Set measurable goals and track progress to ensure continuous improvement.

3. **Promote Ethical Governance:** Foster and support a culture of transparency, accountability, and ethical behavior. Ensure corporate governance practices align with the company's values and long-term vision.

4. **Engage Stakeholders:** Collaborate with stakeholders, including employees, customers, suppliers, and community members, to understand their needs and expectations. Involve them in sustainability initiatives and build strong, mutually beneficial relationships.

5. **Foster Innovation:** Encourage innovation and creativity to develop sustainable products, services, and business models. Support research and development efforts that drive sustainability and long-term growth.

6. **Educate and Inspire:** Educate employees and stakeholders about the importance of sustainability and long-term impact. Inspire them to contribute to the company's vision and take action to create positive change.

Exercise: The Legacy Blueprint Workshop

To help leaders and teams develop and implement strategies for building a sustainable legacy, here is an exercise called the Legacy Blueprint Workshop:

1. **Gather Your Team:** Assemble a diverse group of employees from various departments and levels within the company. This exercise includes considering vendors or customers to get their feedback and perspective.

2. **Define Your Vision:** Begin by defining a long-term vision for the company that emphasizes sustainability, social responsibility, and ethical governance. Consider what you want the company's legacy to be in 10, 20, or even 50 years.

3. **Find Key Areas:** Identify key areas where the company can make a significant impact, such as environmental sustainability, community engagement, employee well-being, and ethical business practices.

4. **Set Goals and Metrics:** Develop specific, measurable goals for each key area. Establish metrics to track progress and ensure accountability.

5. **Develop Action Plans:** Create detailed action plans to achieve the defined goals. Assign responsibilities, set timelines, and distribute resources to support the initiatives.

6. **Engage Stakeholders:** Involve stakeholders in the planning process and seek their input and feedback. Ensure that their perspectives and needs are considered in the legacy blueprint.

7. **Implement and Monitor:** Launch the initiatives and watch their progress regularly. Collect data, assess outcomes, and adjust as needed to stay on track

8. **Celebrate and Share:** Recognize and celebrate achievements and milestones. Share success stories internally and externally to inspire continued commitment and action.

To Ourselves and our Posterity Summary

Building a sustainable and enduring legacy involves adopting a long-term vision, integrating sustainability into business strategy, preserving your culture, and prioritizing ethical governance and social responsibility. By focusing on long-term impact and responsible practices, leaders can create a legacy that benefits current and future generations. Remember, a commitment to sustainability not only enhances the company's reputation and resilience but also contributes to a more just and sustainable world.

In the closing chapter, we will synthesize the principles and practices explored throughout the book and provide a roadmap for leaders to implement these strategies in their organizations. This chapter will help you summarize the key takeaways and offer practical guidance for creating a thriving, resilient, and sustainable business.

CHAPTER 9

Do Ordain and Establish

Those final words of the Preamble are my favorite: Do ordain and Establish. Those are strong words, and they mean the following to me: by ordaining the principles of creating a great culture through Preamble Leadership, we are endorsing them, which is part of the experience. But we must go a step further. We cannot just talk about creating a great culture or endorse Preamble Leadership. We must establish it.

The following Key Principles and Practices will help you design your own process to build your legacy culture. This last chapter synthesizes those exercises not simply to ordain but also to establish. By establishing, we are integrating the system to create a culture that will last the test of time.

The Preamble Leadership Approach

A successful organization is built on a foundation of strong leadership and a holistic approach to managing people, processes, and goals. By integrating the principles discussed in this book, leaders can create a cohesive and legacy culture where employees feel valued, empowered, and motivated to contribute their best.

> *"The most effective way to do it is to do it!"*
>
> *Amelia Earhart*

The Roadmap to Integration

1. We the People: Engaging Every Employee in the Culture

- **Involve Employees in Decision-Making:** Encourage employees to participate in shaping the company culture and decision-making processes. This fosters a sense of ownership and commitment.

- **Promote Feedback and Communication:** Find ways to hear the voice of the employee. Communicate and listen to employees to cultivate a culture that is built for and by the people.

- **Engagement Exercises:** Conduct regular engagement and accountability exercises to strengthen the connection between employees and the organization.

2. Form a More Perfect Union: Aligning People with Culture

- **Cultural Fit:** Ensure that new hires align with the company's values and culture. Use behavioral interviews and personality assessments to identify the right fit.

- **Continuous Alignment:** Regularly assess and realign employees' roles and responsibilities to match their strengths and the company's evolving needs.
- **Development Programs:** Implement development programs that help employees grow and adapt to the company culture.

3. Establish Justice: Defining and Upholding Core Values

- **Core Values:** Clearly define the company's core values and behaviors and integrate them into every facet of across the organization.
- **Fair Treatment:** Ensure that all employees are treated fairly and equitably. Implement policies that promote transparency and accountability.
- **Values Alignment:** Encourage employees to align their personal values with the company's values, creating a cohesive and unified culture.

4. Ensure Domestic Tranquility

- **Support Employee well-being:** Provide both physical and mental health systems for employees to grow and thrive.
- **Foster a Positive Culture:** Ensure the values and behaviors of your culture drive healthy practices not only for your bottom line but also for your employees.
- **Grow your employees:** Provide opportunities for employees to advance and grow within your organization.

5. Provide for the Common Defense: Building Resilient Teams and Systems

- **Market Analysis:** Regularly analyze the competitive landscape to understand external threats and opportunities.
- **Internal Efficiency:** Streamline internal processes and eliminate inefficiencies to strengthen the organization's resilience.
- **Team Building:** Develop resilient teams that can adapt to challenges and collaborate effectively.

6. Promote the General Welfare: Enhancing Employee Well-Being

- **Wellness Programs:** Provide comprehensive wellness programs that address physical, mental, and emotional health.
- **Work-Life Balance:** Promote work-life balance through flexible work arrangements and supportive policies.
- **Community Engagement:** Encourage employees to engage in community service and volunteer activities, enhancing their sense of purpose and connection.

7. Secure the Blessings of Liberty: Empowering Employees

- **Autonomy:** Grant employees the autonomy to make decisions and take ownership of their work.

- **Innovation:** Foster a culture of innovation by encouraging risk-taking and creative thinking.
- **Continuous Learning:** Support continuous learning and development to help employees grow and thrive.

8. To Ourselves and Our Posterity: Building a Sustainable Legacy

- **Sustainability:** Integrate sustainability into the core business strategy, focusing on long-term impact and responsible practices.
- **Ethical Governance:** Promote transparency, accountability, and ethical behavior throughout the organization.
- **Legacy Planning:** Develop a long-term vision that emphasizes sustainability, social responsibility, culture, and enduring success.

We the People, in order to form a more perfect Union, establish Justice and ensure domestic Tranquility, provide for the common Defense, promote the General Welfare, and secure the Blessings of Liberty to ourselves and our Posterity, do ordain and establish these practices!

Conclusion

As we conclude this journey through the principles of "Preamble Leadership," it is essential to remember true leadership is not just about achieving short-term goals but about creating a lasting and positive impact: your legacy. By embracing these principles, leaders can build organizations that are not only successful but are resilient, ethical, and committed to the well-being of their employees, customers, and communities.

I have had the opportunity to work with some of the best leaders in the country and am convinced their attention to their employees is the common thread that binds their leadership success. Your employees will never be better to your customers than you are to your employees. The preamble to great customer service is great employee service, and the preamble to a legacy culture is leadership. Preamble Leadership requires a commitment to continuous improvement, innovation, and responsible stewardship. It is about leaving a legacy on which future generations can build and be proud.

Thank you for embarking on this journey. May your leadership inspire positive change, enduring success, and a legacy that stands the test of time.

Resources

Exercise: Legacy Visioning Workshop

To help leaders and teams envision and create a sustainable legacy, here is an exercise called the Legacy Visioning Workshop:

1. **Gather Your Team:** Bring together a diverse group of leaders and employees from various departments and levels.

2. **Reflect on the Journey:** Begin with a reflection on the principles and practices discussed in this book. Discuss how these have been or can be applied within the organization.

3. **Envision the Future:** Ask participants to envision the organization's legacy 10, 20, and 50 years from now. What impact do they want the company to have on its employees, community, and industry?

4. **Identify Key Actions:** Identify the key actions and initiatives needed to achieve this vision. Prioritize these actions and develop a strategic plan.

5. **Commit to the Vision:** Encourage participants to commit to the vision and take ownership of their roles in creating

the sustainable legacy. Develop individual and team action plans to support the broader strategic goals.

6. **Monitor and Celebrate:** Establish a system for monitoring progress and celebrating milestones. Continuously seek feedback and adjust stay aligned with the vision.

By engaging in this exercise, leaders and teams can collectively envision and create a legacy that reflects the principles of "Preamble Leadership" and secures the blessings of liberty for future generations.

Employee Wellness Assessment

Please answer each question honestly based on your experiences and feelings over the past month. Your responses will help us understand your overall well-being and identify areas where we can provide additional support and resources. Your answers will remain confidential.

Physical Well-Being

1. Exercise Frequency: How often do you engage in physical exercise (e.g., walking, running, gym workouts)?
    5 Daily
    4 Several times a week
    3 Once a week
    2 Rarely
    1 Never

2. Sleep Quality: How would you rate the quality of your sleep over the past month?
    5 Excellent
    4 Good
    3 Fair
    2 Poor
    1 Very Poor

3. Nutrition: How often do you consume a balanced diet that includes fruits, vegetables, proteins, and whole grains?
- 5 Daily
- 4 Several times a week
- 3 Once a week
- 2 Rarely
- 1 Never

4. Energy Levels: How would you rate your overall energy levels during a typical workday?
- 5 Very High
- 4 High
- 3 Moderate
- 2 Low
- 1 Very Low

5. Medical Check-Ups: How often do you go for routine medical check-ups and screenings?
- 5 Annually
- 4 Every few years
- 3 Rarely
- 2 Only when necessary
- 1 Never

Psychological Well-Being

6. Stress Levels: How would you rate your overall stress levels over the past month?
- 5 Very Low
- 4 Low
- 3 Moderate
- 2 High
- 1 Very High

7. Work-Life Balance: How satisfied are you with your current work-life balance?

   5 Very Satisfied
   4 Satisfied
   3 Neutral
   2 Dissatisfied
   1 Very Dissatisfied

8. Mental Health: How often do you feel overwhelmed or unable to cope with your responsibilities?

   5 Never
   4 Rarely
   3 Sometimes
   2 Often
   1 Always

9. Support Systems: Do you feel that you have adequate support from colleagues, friends, or family when dealing with personal or work-related issues?

   5 Always
   4 Often
   3 Sometimes
   2 Rarely
   1 Never

10. Happiness: How often do you feel happy and content with your life?

   5 Always
   4 Often
   3 Sometimes
   2 Rarely
   1 Never

Occupational Well-Being

11. Job Satisfaction: How satisfied are you with your current job role and responsibilities?
- 5 Very Satisfied
- 4 Satisfied
- 3 Neutral
- 2 Dissatisfied
- 1 Very Dissatisfied

12. Work Environment: How would you rate the overall work environment and culture in your workplace?
- 5 Excellent
- 4 Good
- 3 Fair
- 2 Poor
- 1 Very Poor

13. Professional Growth: Do you feel that you have sufficient opportunities for professional growth and development in your current role?
- 5 Always
- 4 Often
- 3 Sometimes
- 2 Rarely
- 1 Never

14. Recognition: How often do you feel recognized and appreciated for your contributions at work?
- 5 Always
- 4 Often
- 3 Sometimes
- 2 Rarely
- 1 Never

15. Workload: How manageable do you find your current workload?
   5 Very Manageable
   4 Manageable
   3 Neutral
   2 Unmanageable
   1 Very Unmanageable

Scoring Rubric for Employee Wellness Assessment

Each question is scored on a scale from 1 to 5, where higher scores indicate better well-being. Total scores will be divided into three categories: Physical Well-Being, Psychological Well-Being, and Occupational Well-Being. Each category will then be summed to give an overall wellness score.

Scoring Scale:

5 points: Most positive response

4 points: Second most positive response

3 points: Neutral response

2 points: Second most negative response

1 point: Most negative response

Total Score Calculation:

Physical Well-Being: Sum of scores for Questions 1-5 (Maximum 25)

Psychological Well-Being: Sum of scores for Questions 6-10 (Maximum 25)

Occupational Well-Being: Sum of scores for Questions 11-15 (Maximum 25)

Overall Wellness Score: Sum of scores for all 15 questions (Maximum 75)

Interpretation of Scores:

Physical, Psychological, and Occupational Well-Being (Each category, out of 25):

21-25: Excellent

16-20: Good

11-15: Fair

6-10: Poor

1-5: Very Poor

Overall Wellness (Out of 75):

61-75: Excellent overall well-being

46-60: Good overall well-being

31-45: Fair overall well-being

16-30: Poor overall well-being

1-15: Very poor overall well-being

Using the Results:

1. **Identify Strengths and Areas for Improvement:** Compare scores across various categories to identify strengths and areas needing improvement.

2. **Targeted Interventions:** Develop and implement interventions and support systems tailored to the needs identified through the assessment.

3. **Monitor Progress:** Conduct regular follow-up assessments to track progress and adjust strategies as necessary.

Company Empowerment Practices Assessment

This assessment framework provides a comprehensive overview of key areas to evaluate when analyzing your team's or company's empowerment practices. It helps identify strengths and areas for improvement to foster a more empowered and engaged workforce. This is a good discussion document to use with your leaders on a regular basis to assess empowerment toward Preamble Leadership.

1. Leadership Commitment

Observation:
Evaluate the extent to which senior leadership visibly supports and champions employee empowerment.

Indicators:

- Leaders regularly communicate the importance of empowerment.
- Empowerment goals are part of the strategic vision and objectives.

2. Decision-Making Autonomy

Observation:
Assess the degree of autonomy employees have in their roles.

Indicators:

- Employees can make decisions without excessive approvals
- There is a clear delegation of authority.

3. Access to Information

Observation:
Determine how easily employees can access the information they need to make informed decisions.

Indicators:

- Availability of relevant data and resources.
- Transparency in communication from top management.

4. *Training and Development*

Observation:
Review the company's commitment to employee growth and skill enhancement.

Indicators:

- Regular training programs focused on decision-making, problem-solving, and leadership.
- Opportunities for continuous learning and development.

5. Recognition and Rewards

Observation:
Examine how the company recognizes and rewards empowered behavior.

Indicators:

- Systems in place to reward initiative and innovation.
- Public acknowledgment of empowered employees' achievements.

6. Feedback Mechanisms

Observation:
Evaluate the processes for providing and receiving feedback.

Indicators:

- Regular performance reviews with a focus on empowerment.
- Open channels for employees to give feedback to management.

7. Culture of Trust

Observation:
Assess the level of trust within the organization.

Indicators:

- Employees feel safe to take risks and make decisions.
- A supportive environment where failures are seen as learning opportunities.

8. Cross-Functional Collaboration

Observation:
Look at the extent of collaboration across different departments.

Indicators:

- Teams are encouraged to work together and share knowledge.
- Projects and initiatives that require cross-departmental cooperation.

9. Inclusive Practices

Observation:
Assess the inclusivity of empowerment practices.

Indicators:

- All employees, regardless of their role or background, have opportunities for empowerment.
- Initiatives that specifically aim to empower underrepresented groups.

10. Measurement and Improvement

Observation:
Evaluate how the company measures the success of its empowerment practices and seeks to improve them.

Indicators:

- Regular assessments and surveys on employee empowerment.
- Action plans based on feedback and assessment results.